What Are You Waiting For?

© 2016 Forward Movement

ISBN 978-880284332

Printed in the USA

Forward
Movement

What Are You Waiting For?

Christine McSpadden

Forward Movement
Cincinnati, Ohio

Table of Contents

PREFACE

The invitation to write this book could not have come at a more opportune time. Asked to write about the theme of waiting for the season of Advent, I felt like an expert on the topic. I recently moved back to the United States from the United Kingdom and have felt like I am waiting in all aspects of my life: waiting to get unpacked, waiting to settle back in, waiting to catch up with friends, waiting to get a job, waiting in relationships, waiting on vocational questions.

In this past year, I have learned many humbling lessons about what it means to wait. I have felt the sharp pain and dull ache of being forced to wait, and I have learned strategies to cultivate patience. I have experienced again what it is to anticipate joy and to hope in more.

I have also felt, poignantly, the importance of waiting to the spiritual life. We only feel the heart-tug of waiting when something matters to us. Otherwise, we remain indifferent, and the passing of time has no particular impact on us. But when we care about something, when it means something to us, when we love someone, our waiting becomes yearning. In a way, we put our physical and emotional selves at the mercy of that for which we wait. We open ourselves in utter vulnerability to another timeline and to another's response.

When we are beholden in this way, our condition mirrors the essence of a God who loves us so much—and to whom we matter so much—that this God would take on the flesh and blood of mortals to come and dwell among us.

God meets the best and worst in us with equal amounts of affection, embracing the fullness of an incarnate world in all its beauty and grittiness, its poetry and messiness, its tragedy and joy. In seeking perfect communion with all creation yesterday, today, and tomorrow, God ever offers a life of more.

I have trusted you, Holy One
*   and waited for you.*

When I was mired in misery
*   you touched me with your spirit.*

You pulled me out
*   and set me on solid ground.*

You put a song in my heart and work in my hands.
*   I praise you.*

I know what you want for me,
*   and where the meaning of my life lies –*
*   Not in rituals, offerings, sacrifices, or creeds,*
*   just my heart; open to others, and open to you.*

I try and live that way.
*   I fail often but you nudge and beckon and I follow.*

I pray that my words, my song, my life
*   show forth your light and light others' way.*

Make all who seek you find you.

Touch us with your spirit, that we may be glad.

–Psalm 40
Psalms for a New World.
Used with permission.

INTRODUCTION

You want something different this year. As the rest of the world gears up for the slog through the winter holiday season, you want to diverge from the pre-Christmas season commercial ramp-up—you want more. You want a season of thoughtfulness and reflection, a sense of depth and purpose. You want to feel joy.

It is easy to get bogged down in the run-up to Christmas Day, inundated by addressing cards, consumed by incessant shopping, driven mad by holiday Muzak, all the while angst-ridden that it won't be enough, that it won't meet expectations. Each year you try another strategy to ease the anxiety: Order everything online, put a moratorium on travel, send digital cards. Yet try as you may, the steady *sturm und drang* sweeps you into its tempest.

The meditations in this book offer something different. And, in reading them this Advent—either alone, meeting regularly with a group, with members of your family, or creating a temporary and intentional online community—you join Christians through the ages and all over the globe who choose a counter-cultural way. They pause. They stop. They wait. They listen. They watch, and they wait some more.

The season of Advent celebrates waiting, in ways simple and sublime, practical and theological. We wait for the birth of

Jesus in a straw-filled barn in the Judean backwater of Bethlehem. We wait for the consummation of the cosmos in the final coming of God's kingdom. We wait for the feast of Christmas and the flesh-and-blood reminder that God sent his beloved Son into the world so that we mortals might have new life and that our future lies open to possibilities beyond what we can ask or imagine.

We rarely think of waiting as a positive experience. Waiting often feels like time wasted, time robbed from things we would rather be doing. So often waiting is filled with dread, anxiety, or confusion. It elicits restlessness, distress, or fear. So often, waiting feels endless or prolonged.

What Are You Waiting For? explores the power and promise in waiting. By opening up the experience of waiting, by thinking about it creatively, and by perceiving it as part of God's invitation to a new reality, this book seeks to transfigure time spent waiting. It is designed for the season of Advent but hopefully will provide a resource to which you might return when you find yourself in a time and place of waiting.

As you begin this book of reflections, you are invited to take apart the question: *What Are You Waiting For?*

What? What is going on in your life, or what is not going on that you hope will change or come to pass? What is unresolved, unknown, or unimaginable?

Why are you waiting? Are you in transition? Are you waiting on someone else to make a decision? Are you waiting for more information, or for things to unfold, for news, for something to change?

How are you in the waiting? Are you anxious, confused, disoriented? Are you expectant, hopeful, curious? Does your waiting feel passive or active?

Where are you? Do you feel like you are moving forward or backward, or like you take a few steps forward and then slip back? Do you feel stuck or in a rut? Do you feel like everything you have tried leads to more of the same result, or do you see productive change ahead on the horizon?

Who is waiting with you? Are you waiting on someone? Do your next steps depend on someone else or others? Do you have companions or support while you wait? Do you have guides? Who has your back? Who is on your team?

When do you think things might change? When do you think you might see resolution? Is there a timeline? Do you see an outcome in sight?

What Are You Waiting For? takes you on a journey through Advent. Each Sunday, you will read a reflection on a topic that is then explored in shorter meditations throughout the week. With four Sundays and the weekdays and Saturdays following them, the season of Advent gives us time to cultivate fruitful anticipation in our hearts and minds, our daily lives, and our relationships. For these four weeks—plus a few days more or less depending on the year—we have the opportunity to contemplate time differently.

We are part of a much bigger story unfolding in real time within an eternal, cosmic context. The story stretches over millennia but takes place in nanoseconds. Each moment offers a new opportunity to choose life. And that new life is waiting for us.

First Sunday of Advent

Time

*But do not ignore this one fact, beloved,
that with the Lord one day is like a thousand years,
and a thousand years are like one day.*

—2 Peter 3:8

Time. It has an elastic quality. An hour can drag on with boredom or dread for what seems like an eternity. A year can fly by with excitement, and we wonder where it went. We perceive time moving forward, backward, and standing still.

The Greeks helped us think about time in two modes. The first is *kairos*—or time outside of time, eternal time, sometimes called God's time. The word *kairos* can be translated as "the right moment," the propitious moment for decision or action. When the time is right, we are in *kairos*.

The second mode of time is called *chronos*—measured time, ticking time, by which we set our clocks, schedule our appointments, and bill hours. We watch the wall clock or wait for the chimes of the grandfather clock in the hallway or the

14

cuckoo clock in the den. The o'clocks, the "of the clocks" time, is measured by precise pendulum weights and laser cut gems. We strap clocks to our wrists, attach them to chains tucked into pockets, or suspend them on necklaces as pendants. We call these clocks "watches" because we can watch *chronos* time passing.

Yet whether we regard time as *kairos* or *chronos*, it cannot be parceled up. Time is a strange phenomenon. It resists our efforts to organize it in any foolproof way. No one has been able to nail down time.

Think about a day. When does it start? Astronomers from the second century through to 1925 thought a day ran from noon to noon instead of midnight to midnight. The Babylonians and Greeks timed the new day from sunset. Jews still do. The Christian Church structured the day around the canonical hours meted out in threes, which recall the passion of Christ: Matins, Lauds, Prime, Terce, Sext, None, Vespers, and Compline.

Days string together as weeks. A week runs from Saturday to Saturday for those celebrating the sabbath on that day and for vacation rental properties. For Christians, a week spans Sunday to Sunday, an eight-day cycle in which Sunday, as the day of resurrection, represents the eighth day.

Weeks are bundled into months. In the Mediterranean region, weeks were gathered according to the lunar cycle. But a lunar cycle is twenty-eight days, leaving twenty-nine and one-quarter days floating around. So Ethiopians decided to have thirteen months. Much of the Western world parceled the time into twelve months.

But you run into problems by the second month because 365 days and a quarter add another full day every four years. Western calendars observe a leap year by arbitrarily adding one day to the end of every fourth February.

The church eschewed months altogether and divided its year into liturgical seasons. From Advent—which begins the ecclesiastical new year—through the Last Sunday after Pentecost, the seasons recall the preparation for birth, life, death, resurrection, and ascension of Jesus.

Many others have opted out of the standard twelve-month calendar, from the Baha'is, Bengalis, and Bikram Samvats to the Sufis, Tibetan Buddhists, and Zoroastrians. Can we blame them? It's hard to believe that such a precarious system actually dominates global markets, locates events in world history, and dictates how many candles you have on your birthday cake.

It's just as dubious if you measure time the other way, breaking an hour into sixty minutes, sixty minutes into sixty seconds, seconds into milliseconds and nanoseconds until you end up with immeasurable increments of time, liquidated and slipping through your fingers like a Salvador Dali wristwatch.

Yet these droplets of a day add up to a life lived; these atomistic moments combine to make up lives inhabited. The space sandwiched between before and after—the interstitial space of the present, is where we live and breathe and have our true being. Nanosecond to nanosecond. Minute to minute. Day by day. These are the moments that change us.

Experiment this week:

Notice time. Take note of when time seems longer, when it seems shorter. What is happening? How does elongated time make you feel? Is it positive or negative? How does time that seems to go by faster feel? Is it positive or negative? What is happening? Do you see patterns? What does this awareness of time suggest to you?

Consider a way that you might mark time this season in a way that you can see: lighting candles, using an Advent calendar, or adding greenery or flowers to an Advent arrangement.

Propitiousness

*For everything there is a season,
and a time for every matter under heaven...*

–Ecclesiastes 3:1

From the Book of Ecclesiastes—or Qohelet, meaning the teacher, the preacher—these words from Hebrew wisdom literature are traditionally attributed to King Solomon in his old, sage age. Yet they were probably composed in the third century BCE when Hellenistic kings from Egypt oppressed the Jews of Judea.

Those studying the *Tanakh*,[1] or the Hebrew Bible, were required to wait to read Ecclesiastes until after they were seasoned scholars. The book's existential themes were deemed too complex for the neophyte and required the discerning maturity of age to be properly understood.

---

1 The word Tanakh is the term used for the Hebrew Bible. The term is formed by the beginning sounds of the three sections of Hebrew Scripture: the Law, or Torah (Tɔ); the Prophets, or Ne'va'im (nah); and the Writings, or Ket'u'vim (kh).

The book's blunt and somewhat resigned tone provides a corrective to excessive self-assurance. Self-assurance suggests that we are in control. Yet so many of the biggest moments of our lives lie outside our control—when we will find love, when a child will be born, when we will fall sick, when a depression will lift, when we will die. With a few exceptions, these big events elude our mortal control.

With the statement "for everything there is a season," Qohelet affirms the belief in *kairos*, that there is an auspicious or right time for things to unfold and occur. This idea is different from the popular wisdom that everything happens for a reason. In fact, the Book of Ecclesiastes says just the opposite: Most things don't happen for a reason; they are vanity *(hevel)*, vapor, breath, emptiness. Indeed, according to the teacher, everything is *hevel*. Things happen, to be sure, yet it is our response to them that matters. And things do happen propitiously, which is to say we will hear when we are ready to hear. We will understand when our minds are open to understanding. We will desist from denial when our hearts are prepared to accept the full truth.

I recently started wearing reading glasses. I haven't been able to see far away since third grade, but now I cannot see close up either. After long denying my worsening hyperopia, I finally gave in when I couldn't read menus or the printed prayers to lead them. It took time to accept the truth of my eyes' degeneration. I had to wait until I was ready to accept that truth before I could act. Now in full acceptance mode, I have joined the ranks who cannot remember where they last laid their glasses!

There is a time for every matter under heaven. Sometimes we have to wait until we are ready to accept a new truth. We need time before we are ready to buy the bifocals, take the last drink, accept a criticism, or forgive a friend.

The time it takes to get there invites us to do the holy work of waiting. This holy work of waiting allows us to gain clarity, motivation, a measure of acceptance, and the ability to remember and still forgive.

God with Us

Lord, you have searched me out and known me.

–Psalm 139:1a

At five minutes to five, bells chime, summoning us to Evensong. At one minute to the hour, they stop their exuberant chiming. Then, sixty seconds of silence. Inside the nave of the soaring cathedral the procession waits in position. The choir stands under the back edge of the great dome ready to sing the Introit. From the silence tolls a deep A-flat: *Bong, bong, bong, bong, bong.*

Great Tom tolls the hour. Five deep, resonant rings. Tom resides in the southwest tower of St. Paul's Cathedral in London. Tom is not the biggest bell though. That would be Great Paul. Paul is so big that the roads of London had to be widened for the 16½ tons to make it through the city on a steam trailer in 1882.

I'm living on the close of St. Paul's Cathedral in staff housing—a simply furnished room of a beautiful brick and stone building the dean jokingly calls the "rabbit hutch." The bells structure my day and infuse my sleep—tolling on the hour, chiming on the quarter-hour, calling us to prayer. The bells are synchronized to the giant Smith of Derby clock mechanism. Housed in its 18-foot flatbed frame, the weight-driven mechanism with gravity escapement, fitted with an electric winding system, ticks off the minutes. Watching the carefully calibrated and oiled gears turn with precision, it feels like I've been shrunk down to the size of a speck, thrust into the innards of a wristwatch.

The Deists thought of God as a great clockmaker who created the cosmos, wound it up, and then left it to run on its own without (divine) interference. This impersonal image of God persists today.

Yet Christians proclaim the opposite. The Christian way confesses a God intimately involved in human life. This God does not leave us to our own devices but accompanies us in joy and sorrow. Known by the name *Emmanuel*, this God is with us through exciting heights and debilitating lows, for better or worse, until the end of the age. This God chooses to enter into the beauty and vulgarity of enfleshed life, surrendering to be profoundly contained, constrained, and affected by this world— this choice is the miracle we await again during Advent.

This God acts in *chronos* to bring us into the sacred life of the divine and into *kairos* in ways relational, loving, and passionate.

Patience

*Lead me in your truth, and teach me, for you are the
God of my salvation; for you I wait all day long.*

–Psalm 25:5, NRSV

Time heals all wounds. It will get better over time. It just takes
time. You'll get there in time. Be patient.

When I have to wait, these sayings drive me crazy! They are the
last things I want to hear. I want my pain to end now. I want to
know right this minute. I want it over this instant. Now. I don't
want to have to wait for some later time.

Patience is a virtue—one of the seven great virtues. I served at
a beautiful Anglo-Catholic parish in New Haven, Connecticut,
after graduating from seminary. Seven mosaics graced the floor.
In each of the seven round medallions, tiny earth-toned tesserae
surrounded the Latin word for each of these virtues: Chastity,
Temperance, Charity, Diligence, Kindness, Humility, and
Patience—*Patientia*.

Patience might be a virtue, but it is not one that comes easily to me. More often than not, I find myself swimming against the tide of waiting, crashing into the waves instead of riding them out to where they will take me over time.

I have been rereading works by Simone Weil. Her vantage point seems particularly relevant in this post-Christendom world where many claim to be "spiritual but not religious." Born in the early 1900s into an agnostic Jewish family in Paris, she came to Christianity through the mentoring of a priest and a writer and through her own mystical experience. Though deeply attracted to Christianity, she eschewed baptism her whole life. She loved the worship, rites, ceremony, and theology of the church but was suspicious of the institution. Her suspicion mirrors that of many people today. Her angst parallels that of this age.

In her work *Waiting on God*, Weil writes letters to her mentor Father Perrin, O.P., in which she lays out the idea central to her faith: We are to love God by attending to God. By waiting attentively on God with love, we enact our greatest vocation. Indeed, she goes so far as to say that waiting lies at the heart of Christian spirituality. When we wait, we relinquish control to God's will. In waiting we enact trust in the divine. Waiting releases us from the pressures and temptations of this world—it opens us to the creativity of the Creator.

Weil speaks of "de-creation," by which she means a state of contemplation whereby we "get out of the way" and let God's radiance shine in and through us. De-creation "undoes the creature in us." We ourselves are obstacles and must consent to withdraw in order to make way for God.[2] She talks about the joy that comes with moving out of the way: "Such a soul… swims in the sea of joy—that is in the sea of delights flowing and streaming from the Divinity, and she herself feels no joy for she herself is joy, and swims and floats in joy without feeling any joy because she inhabits Joy and Joy inhabits her."[3]

While I don't always feel like I experience joy while I wait, I can imagine and long for joy. And I am willing to wait.

2 Simone Weil, *Gravity and Grace* (London and New York: Routledge, 2002), 32-39.
3 Ibid.

Breaking the Fourth Wall

For [Christ Jesus] is our peace;
in his flesh he has made both groups into one
and has broken down the dividing wall.

–Ephesians 2:14

Hi there. I'm glad you're back and reading this meditation. I am tricking you a little bit, playing with space and time. I am breaking down the "fourth wall" of the writer's objective stance and addressing you directly.

This boundary-breaking technique is used often in modern, realistic theatre. Three walls set the stage, and the fourth wall opens to the audience. Plays that have their characters break out of the "box" and acknowledge their own fictitiousness, speaking directly to the audience, employ this technique of breaking down the fourth wall. Think Puck in Shakespeare's *A Midsummer Night's Dream*, the narrator in *Our Town*, Francis Underwood in *House of Cards*, and Ferris in *Ferris Bueller's Day Off*.

I am breaking down the fourth wall to illustrate two things. First, space and time can be malleable, taking different forms depending on our perspective. But then, so many things take different forms depending on our perspective. From one place, we can feel like insiders and from another, outsiders. In a certain situation, we can feel on top of our problems or buried by them. We can feel a sense of agency, like some things are within our control, and we can feel victimized, like everything is beyond our control. Waiting can become something more enjoyable and enriching. Waiting opens us up to be transfigured by grace.

Secondly, I am intrigued by the insight that breaking down the fourth wall imitates the way God works in our lives. We act out our dramas, striving to stay on script. We try to keep everyone else on our script too, but they keep going off book! They steal the scene or forget their lines or write their own scripts. And in the midst of all that bungled drama, God enters into our walled existence, breaks down the barriers, reminds of us our own hardened narratives, and acknowledges our very real humanity. God incarnate, the long-awaited Messiah, meets us in the flesh over and over again, beyond the boundaries of time and space. Then from our limited perspectives, God expands the view, broadening and enlivening the vista before us.

First Friday of Advent

The Unexpected

*On this day the L*ORD *has acted;*
we will rejoice and be glad in it.

—Psalm 118:24

I love road trips. I love the sound of the highway thrumming as I cover ground. I love stopping at gas stations and treating myself to Slurpees and Cheetos. I love driving without a map, carefree about my destination. I love being lulled by the passing landscape in the moment.

Ever since I was a little girl I have relished road trips. Maybe it's about enjoying the journey for its own sake, even when I don't know exactly where I am going. Maybe it's about seeing where the road takes me and stumbling on unexpected delights along the way. Maybe it's about leaving behind one place, not quite knowing what awaits me, and appreciating what's right in front of me now.

I tend to take up residence in the future or the past, less so in the present. Yet the future and the past are habitations merely in our minds. So why do we spend so much time in these figment-of-our-imagination locations? Dwelling on or ruing the past, dreading or yearning for the future?

I've realized that in good times, I enjoy reminiscing and delight in daydreaming, anticipating what might lie just ahead on the horizon.

But in difficult times, I have figured out ways to avoid the present by shuttling between the already and the not yet. Both tendencies lead to a form of denial. In those time-bending, headroom spaces, I can deny my feelings and cut myself off from responsibility, waiting to be rescued or somehow saved by outside forces. I employ copious amounts of mental energy numbing myself to the present and avoiding action.

Waiting requires that I keep intentionally pushing myself to inhabit the present. I have to think about making myself available to what is in front of me, in the moment. The season of Advent reminds me to live each day for what it uniquely holds.

Cranking up my tunes, I drive south on Highway 101. The Pacific surf crashes on the shoreline off to the right. Caught up in thought, I resolve to learn from the past and to plan and dream for the future. I recommit myself to dwell in, and engage with, the present. I'll try enjoying the journey for its own sake, even when I don't know exactly where I'm headed, looking for unexpected delights along the way.

I'm getting hungry, and my car needs gas. The next exit is 191A Pismo National Beach. I turn onto the off-ramp and drive down toward the strip of tattoo parlors and little seaside motels. Lo and behold, what do I see before me but Old West Cinnamon Rolls! I park, get out, and get in line. They have nine different kinds of cinnamon rolls. The pecan one has my name on it.

Thank you, God, for unexpected delights of the present moment.

Movement in Waiting

*Now to him who by the power at work within us
is able to accomplish abundantly far more
than all we can ask or imagine, to him be glory
in the church and in Christ Jesus
to all generations, forever and ever. Amen.*

–Ephesians 3:20-21

Waiting is movement.

I am waiting to start the wedding procession. I have checked on and prayed with the bride and her party. I've lined up the groomsmen and taken my place to lead them to the altar. I track the second hand on my watch as it approaches the top of the hour, a sacred hour to be marked and kept in God's time and the moment that begins a new life for this couple.

Chronological time passes. The second-hand clicks. The pendulum shifts to to fro. Electronic clocks synchronized to satellites roll to the next digit. The interstitial space between now and the next *now* collapses. This moment in time is different from the one preceding it. Waiting in real time involves movement.

When you're feeling stuck, this fact sheds light on another perspective. There is movement in the stuck-ness! No matter how tiny, how undetectable, something is happening to move things forward. Something has already begun and progresses on a trajectory. Waiting, we sit in the arc of that trajectory while being carried forward in time. Therefore, in the words of theologian Henri Nouwen, each advancing moment is "never a movement from nothing to something but always a movement from something to something more."[4]

A priest friend of mine tells the story of a parishioner whose faith in Christ had deepened and who had become much more involved in the parish. Thinking that this parishioner's story might be inspirational to others in the congregation, my friend asked this woman if she would preach one Sunday and tell the story of her deepening faith.

After much coaxing, the woman finally agreed. The morning of her sermon she sat in the front row. When the time came to preach, she stood up, went to the pulpit without notes, stared out at the people, cleared her throat, and said, "My friends, I just have one thing to say to you." Everyone in the pews waited with bated breath for her to reveal her wisdom. And she said, "I want you to know that there is always more." And she sat down.

---

4 Henri Nouwen, *A Spirituality of Waiting: Being Alert to God's Presence in Our Lives* (Notre Dame, Indiana: Ave Maria Press, 2006).

With God there is always more. By divine nature, the reconciliation, creativity, and love that continually happen in God continually happen in the moments of God's time, for God is all in all. When we don't just sit there, and even when we *do* just sit there, we are caught up in God's time, moving from grace to grace.

SECOND SUNDAY OF ADVENT:

Passive Waiting/Contemplation

We love because he first loved us.

−1 John 4:19

Inevitably, we wait. We wait in the womb to be born. We wait to grow to the next developmental milestone. We wait for our next birthday, for Christmas Day, or for a trip. We wait in line, for test results, for phone calls. We wait to hear from search committees and lawyers and loved ones. We wait to move on from our past, and we wait to move into our future.

In *Waiting*, a children's book and winner of the Caldecott Medal, author Kevin Henkes writes about five toys sitting on a windowsill expectantly. The owl looks out the window longing for the moon. The pig waits for the rain. The bear, for the wind. The puppy, for the snow. And the rabbit? The rabbit just looks out the window because he likes to wait! And he's glad enough to be in the company of the others.

This simple book tells a profound truth: If we have to wait, there's no greater way to pass the time than waiting in the presence of love. The practice of waiting in the presence of love is called contemplation.

As traditionally understood, Christian contemplation, or *theoria*, means "the gaze of faith." German theologian, philosopher, and mystic Meister Eckhart describes the gaze of faith in this way: "The eye through which I see God is the same eye with which God sees me; my eye and God's eye are one eye, one sight, one knowledge, and one love."[5] Contemplation, then, involves receiving the divine gaze and returning it—"love returning love," as Saint Francis of Assisi says.

Contemplation relieves one of all effort. It is passive because it relieves humans from intellectual reflection and activity—as a "wordless awareness and love that we ourselves cannot initiate or prolong."[6]

Yet while the prayer is passive, the heart, mind, body, and soul respond through sensations of union, fusion, immersion, and communion through an experiential apprehension of God's presence. We love in response because we are loved. Contemplation originates in the divine—a reflective dynamic of love is set in motion, lover and beloved mirroring love back and forth over and over.

---

5   Eckhart von Hochheim O.P., from *Sermons of Meister Eckhart*, (c.1260–c.1328).
6   Thomas Dubay S.M., *Fire Within: St. Teresa of Avila, St John of the Cross, and the Gospel on Prayer* (San Francisco: Ignatius Press, 1989), Chapter 5.

In his book, *Finding Your Strength in Difficult Times: A Book of Meditations,* psychiatrist and radio talk show host David Viscott writes:

> The purpose of life is to discover your gift.
> The work of life is to develop it.
> The meaning of life is to give your gift away.[7]

If we take this to be true, then waiting becomes a profound act of giving ourselves over to discernment, grace, and love. No matter our circumstances, whether we feel confusion, anxiety, apprehension, or shame, contemplation shifts the attention from ourselves to God. And in making that shift, we suspend any vestiges of self-recrimination and rest in the beatitude of God. This makes all the difference in the quality of our waiting. Like the little rabbit at the window, we might come to enjoy this time of anticipation.

Experiment this week:

Practice contemplation. You may wish to set apart a specific time. Or you may wish to practice the presence of God in the midst of your day, even while you are busy with other things.

If you choose to do this, start with two minutes and add more time as you wish. Set a timer so that you won't have to worry about the time as it ticks by. Sit comfortably and imagine dwelling in the presence of God. Simply be present. Amid the

---

7 David S. Viscott, *Finding Your Strength in Difficult Times: A Book of Meditations* (Chicago: Contemporary Books of Chicago, 1993), p. 87.

busyness and all that needs to be done this time of year, do nothing but allow God's love to wash over you. You may have thoughts and images that come into your mind. Try to let them go. You might choose to journal afterward, recording your feelings as the week moves forward.

Alternately, focus intentionally on being in the presence of God in the midst of doing other things: washing dishes, waiting at a stoplight, taking a shower, waiting in line. Claim this time (kairos) within time (chronos) to be in God's presence. Notice how waiting feels in these moments and what thoughts arise.

SECOND MONDAY OF ADVENT

Hoping In

I wait for the LORD; my soul waits for him;
in his word is my hope. My soul waits for the LORD,
more than watchmen for the morning,
more than watchmen for the morning.

–Psalm 130:4-5

The idea of waiting is so central to the spiritual life that the psalmist describes it twice in Psalm 130, using the poetic device of magnification. Images of waiting pervade the Old and New Testaments. Waiting characterizes the lives of many saints, and their forbearance in the midst of pain and suffering often undergirds their feats of faith.

Twentieth-century theologian Henri Nouwen goes so far as to say that waiting is essential to the spiritual life.[8] Simone Weil takes it a step further, saying that waiting patiently in expectation is "the foundation of the spiritual life."

---

8 Henri Nouwen, *"A Spirituality of Waiting"* (Indiana: Ave Maria Press, 2006). This reflection draws on Nouwen's article and audiotape about waiting.

Why is waiting so important for the spiritual life? Patient waiting as contemplation cultivates three particular behaviors. First, one who waits with intentionality dwells in the present moment. Letting go of the past and resisting a rush to the future, we apprehend better the full potential of the here and now. The present is not an empty placeholder but rather is a place where possibilities are held, imagined, and considered.

Second, we are able to wait because we can imagine something ahead that is worth moving toward. We feel some measure of hope *in* something—even if it's only the slightest inkling. As opposed to hoping *for* something, which can suck us into fantasy and wishful thinking, hoping in an outcome, person, or situation relates to fidelity and confidence. We can hope in something we trust. I wish for certain Christmas gifts. I hope in God's ability to give me gifts to use for God's glory and that I might receive from the wealth of such divinely bestowed gifts of others. As the psalmist says in Psalm 62:6, "For God alone my soul in silence waits; truly, my hope is in him."

Third, waiting reminds us that we are not in control. Things don't always happen according to our schedule or for our comfort. We must forgo the illusion that life can be managed—that there is some grand timeline to which we must adhere. Intentional waiting means surrendering to surprise, curiosity, and the unexpected. Sure, we all have our life scripts, but others—including God—have them too.

Years ago, I saw a play called *The Mystery of Edwin Drood*. It had several endings, and the audience for the evening picked which ending they wanted. The actors went along with the will of the audience. Similarly, we plan our future, but sometimes forces beyond our control lead to different conclusions. We open ourselves to the presence of God by waiting intentionally, acknowledging the potential of the present, hoping in what is to come (and that something *is*, in fact, coming), and surrendering the illusion of control.

SECOND TUESDAY OF ADVENT

Incubation

Very truly, I tell you, unless a grain of wheat
falls into the earth and dies,
it remains just a single seed;
but if it dies, it bears much fruit.

–John 12:24

I'm in second grade. My teacher Mrs. Phillips—a cherubic-faced, stout woman with hair like Wilma Flintstone—hands out clear plastic cups to each student. She invites us over to a yellow tub of potting soil to spoon into our cups. She gives each of us five butter beans to press into the dirt. We water the planted beans and place the cups on the windowsill to soak up the red-hot Georgia sun.

About five days later, tender shoots push through the soil. Along the clear sides of the cup, I can see taproots legging their way underground. For five days, I imagine my little germinating beans buried in earthen darkness—still, inert, waiting. Unbeknownst to me, they are soaking in sun from the sky, nutrients from the soil, and moisture from watering, and they metabolize everything in a miraculous act of transfiguration.

I think of those little butter beans in moments of darkness, when I feel buried by disappointment, depression, or betrayal. Most times, I cannot see the possibility of new life with my eyes, or know it with my thoughts, or feel it in my body. But in that fertile darkness, I am quenched with living waters and nourished by grace while God's face shines upon me.

Growth takes time though. Problems are not easily metabolized. We need time to let the fullness of a new landscape unfold after disappointment, to find shards of hope in depression, or to reorient ourselves after betrayal. The quality of our waiting seems passive.

So too, holy light, water, and food are not metabolized instantly. They need to be broken down into smaller increments so that their energy is released with its power to transform.

God who first loved so that we can love works on us when we feel weary, when we cannot see a way forward. Like the prophets who groaned in the darkness and were transfigured by their waiting for a great light, we incubate in the darkness. And little by little our efforts stir. Even when we never could have imagined being able to move again, some small shift opens a crack within us, allowing an outside energy to nourish us. We germinate as we wait in the darkness.

Overcoming Paralysis

Stand up, take your mat and walk.

—John 5:8

Time and space lie open before me, but I cannot seem to get past this rut. In this season, the stuck feeling can result from all the things I need to get done; I feel immobilized by the hype of the holidays, the press of demands. More generally, I feel the paralysis of wanting to feel a joy that seems inaccessible.

I cannot get to that great openness ahead that waits for me, pregnant with possibility. I imagine that I am debilitated by illness like the man ailing by the pool at Beth-zatha, taking up my scorned spot each day waiting to be saved. I long to take up my mat and walk. But as yet, I am paralyzed, doomed to lie here in the relentless scorching sun.

I know three things contribute to my paralysis: fear, denial, and self-deception.

Fear: I want to trust that things will get better, but I know they may get worse first. How bad will it get? How much more pain will I have to endure? How much more pain *can* I endure? Will I break? It's tempting to act or to act out. I want to hurry things along. When I feel wronged, I want to lash out. Longing to be anywhere but stuck here, I vacillate between wishing to fight or to flee. The more fearful I feel, the more excruciating the waiting becomes.

Denial: I am not ready to take in the fullness of my situation. It is too scary. It is too painful. It is too disorienting. Like a heavy meal, it takes a while to digest. I can only metabolize small bits at a time. Like Scarlett O'Hara in Margaret Mitchell's *Gone With the Wind*, there are times I say, "I can't think about that right now. I'll go crazy. I'll think about that tomorrow."

Self-deception: I find that I'm unable to face my responsibility in matters full-on. Because I can only bear my defects and misdeeds in small portions, I minimize the magnitude of my transgressions. I play the victim. I think magically. I shrink my world to my problems—what a tiny, arid, and boring world that is. I feel *entitled* to a savior.

I lie on my itchy mat, chafing and exposed under the hot sun—a refining fire of light.

Like Jesus walking by in the story, saving grace comes my way. And the more resentment and self-deception I am willing to shed, the more space there is for divine grace to seep inside. Bit by bit, I metabolize my situation. The more I consume, the less it consumes me. The more I take in, the larger and more comprehensive I allow my perspective to become. I begin trying to discern between what I have the courage to take on and what lies outside my control. I am better able to choose what fits *me*—the person God created—to realize fullness, dignity, and integrity.

I relinquish the desire to control, to strike first. I get past that initial survival instinct—that aggressive, self-centered, destructive fight-or-flight reaction. I respond from the banquet table of resources I have at my disposal and blossom out of the narrow confines of self alone.

My fear subsides. By the grace of God, I take up my mat and walk.

The Word is Very Near You

I will put my law within them,
and I will write it on their hearts.

–Jeremiah 31:33b

The Passionist nuns came over from Italy in the 1700s and settled in Erlanger, Kentucky, by way of Pittsburgh. For decades they have made communion hosts—those thin, tasteless little wafers that many churches rely on for the eucharist because they defy mold. In the YouTube video that documents their manufacturing—uh, I mean cooking—process, Sister Mary Angela greets us at the door and takes us to the kitchen. But first she changes into a light blue habit because the flour wreaks havoc on her black one.

She mixes the batter of flour and water. That's it—just those two ingredients. I am not sure whether the batter, which has the same ingredients as glue, is gross or theologically poetic: It is the glue that binds us. The batter is poured on a griddle stove like a waffle iron; it is pressed, cooked, and trimmed to a large, round bread sheet before being dampened overnight in a humidifier, so it can be cut into individual wafers without cracking.

Sister Mary Angela notes that when she presses the batter in the griddle, it is imprinted by the top metal plate with the symbol of the Chi-Rho (χρ), the first two Greek letters for the word "Christ." The metal plate inscribes this symbol for Christ, the Word of God, while the Almighty asks us to inscribe—to write—the Word of God on our hearts.[9] As the batter is poured out, prayed over, fashioned into holy bread, and impressed with the sign of Christ, so too are we marked as Christ's own each time we take the wafers into our mouths.

I sit in the presence of a communion wafer consecrated earlier during Holy Eucharist. The wafer is displayed in the round, crystal eye of a monstrance—a beautiful gold vessel used to hold a blessed host, the Body of Christ, the Bread of Heaven. As I keep vigil, waiting with this holy food, I contemplate these things.

---

9 Several passages of scripture reference this thought, including: Deuteronomy 6:5–7; 11:18; 30:11–14; Psalm 40:7, 8; 119:11; Proverbs 3:3–6; 4:20–23; 7:1-3; Isaiah 51:7; Jeremiah 31:31–34; Romans 10:4-17; 2 Corinthians 3:2, 3; Hebrews 8:10–12; 10:4–10.

Second Friday of Advent

Excavation

*O tarry and await the LORD's pleasure; be strong,
and he shall comfort your heart; wait patiently for the LORD.*

–Psalm 27:18

I am afraid.

I am stuck. I can't go back in time, and I am not sure I want to go forward. I am stuck in a rut, unable to act. I am waiting.

I get to this stymied place with friendships, jobs, significant others, and my vocation. On most occasions, I just need a recalibration, and time spent in this snarled place becomes a pit stop. But other times it stretches on, becoming long, painful, and all-consuming. A full stop. It feels disheartening and debilitating. Paralyzing. I realize that I cannot rush the resolution, control the contributing factors, or reach the conclusion on a timeline. I feel like I am spiraling down.

Yet I have found from experience that even though I never believe it will happen again, when the spiraling becomes spinning, even then, I eventually hit a solid bottom. And God is there, present in that place.

One summer I worked on an archaeological dig in Beit She'an with the Israel Antiquities Authority. The section I excavated held seventeen layers of civilizations, one built on top of the other, from the contemporary village through the reigns of Kings David and Solomon, and all the way back to the Late Neolithic Age (5000–6000 BCE). Most days as I dug down carefully through the hard, parched earth, I found millennia-old rubbish—sheep bones, broken pottery, discarded oil lamps. Every once in a while I found real treasures—an alabaster doorstop, a signet ring.

Each day required hard, physical labor under the relentless, blazing sun. Dust and dirt kicked up with eddies of wind. Our drinking water almost boiled from the heat by midday. But each day was still exciting—I didn't know what I might find down there in the dirt. And the deeper I went, the more connected I became to those who had gone before me.

In times of waiting when I start spiraling down, I try to remember digging in Beit She'an. I imagine doing the hard work of going deeper in my personal excavation. I am going to find a ton of trash down there, but I will also find precious and valuable jewels. Looked at in this light, my waiting feels more like a creative and expectant time than punishment in a pit. And as I meet grace in that solid bottom, my barrenness becomes fruitfulness.

Discernment

Rejoice in hope, be patient in suffering,
persevere in prayer.

–Romans 12:12

There is a time to act, and there is a time to wait. It may be very hard to know the difference. Acting before it's time—taking control of the situation and forcing things—often backfires. So often we seize control of a situation to our detriment, or the detriment of others.

I learned this hard fact as a child. My friend Reenie and I found a cocoon attached to a branch in her backyard when we were four years old. I knew from my storybooks that a butterfly was inside, and we were curious to peek at this beautiful creature. With our tiny fingers, we carefully pried open the silky threads of the cocoon. Inside we found a fat worm—a pupa, not what we were expecting at all. We made a soft little bed for it in a box, placed it carefully inside, and kept vigil. Alas, we had arrested its development, and it died.

Knowing when to act and when to wait requires discernment and trust—two qualities that can be hard to uphold when we are feeling impatient or out of control! Reinhold Niebuhr's classic *Serenity Prayer* acknowledges this aspect of timing and control: "God, grant me the serenity to accept the things I cannot change, the courage to change the things I can, and the wisdom to know the difference."

Prayer can be our greatest ally while we wait. When I say "prayer," I am including any kind of intentional communication or awareness of God's presence—offered or received. These prayers can be the formulaic, written ones as well as those expressed in breath, movement, and meditation.

Nicholas Herman, otherwise known as Brother Lawrence, was born to a poor family in Lorraine, France, in 1611. After working as a soldier and as a household servant, he joined a Carmelite order in Paris. There, he remained a kitchen servant his entire life, dubbing himself the "lord of all pots and pans." For him, all work was holy work. No task was too trivial to use as a tool for God's companionship. He says, "The time of business does not with me differ from the time of prayer, and in the noise and clatter of my kitchen...I possess God in as great tranquility as if I were on my knees at the blessed sacrament."[10]

From waiting in line at a store to waiting for a loved one to come out from surgery, every place—no matter how majestic or mundane, every time, whether extraordinary or ordinary, every

---

10 Brother Lawrence, *The Practice of the Presence of God* (Old Tappan, NJ: Revell, 1958), 9.

situation, whether clamorous or serene—can be an occasion for prayer.

Prayer takes us out of our own egocentricity. It invites movement and relationship. It infuses impatience with outward-looking content. It helps us discern the pace for action and the timeline for waiting. Prayer reminds us that we are not alone.

Active Waiting

In 1939, after the outbreak of World War II, the Ministry of Information in London began designing morale-boosting posters to be displayed across the British Isles. Set against bold backgrounds, posters designed and produced by Her Majesty's Stationary Office included peppy lines like "Freedom is in Peril" and "Your Courage, Your Cheerfulness, Your Resolution Will Bring Us Victory."

The most famous slogan experienced a revival after a poster that had evaded pulpification turned up in a pile of dusty books headed for auction. The slogan on this poster read, "Keep Calm and Carry On." It has become ubiquitous in souvenir and curio shops the world over. Indeed, it has become so popular that there is now an app for it. With the *Keep Calm Creator*, you can, "Keep Calm and (fill in the blank)."

In blocky lettering, the original poster proclaims a message of forbearance in the face of great danger, loss, and anxiety. Without denying real peril and pathos, it encourages us to cultivate peace and calm, even in the midst of chaos and upheaval. In essence, the reminder to keep calm and carry on bids us to bide our time in the tumult and terror while a part of us remains free from the uncertainty all around us. Ideally, the more we flex muscles of fortitude, the stronger they become, and the less we find ourselves at the mercy of whatever is happening around us.

It is hard to know what one would do as the German Luftwaffe flew overhead dropping their loads. But with paternal and providential cheerleading, the posters aimed to create a reflective spirit in the hearts of the people so they could respond out of experience and wisdom rather than react with rashness. In this act of encouragement, the Ministry hoped to maintain a common national ethos of civility and dignity, even with bombs bursting in air.

Although it may be to a different degree than war, we weather our own withering fire and exploding bombs. We need to find ways to keep moving forward even as restiveness rages around us and when we have to carry on while waiting. It may take more than a poster or snappy slogan to cultivate forbearance in the face of our personal firestorms, yet the inclination to do so benefits us no less.

The practice of keeping calm and carrying on creates space between our outer turmoil and our inner soul. This space allows us to develop intentional patience instead of impatience, a rich repertoire of responsiveness rather than reactivity, pondered thoughtfulness instead of haste.

We hear and sing the words, "Silent Night, Holy Night, all is calm, all is bright" this season of Advent. But we may feel anything but calm and bright. Yet a spiritual practice of keeping calm and carrying on creates a protected place of quiet, stillness, and peace. In some measure, you determine what you will allow in and what gets filtered out. In words attributed to Saint Francis: Patience begets patience. The more you practice creating a calm space within yourself, the more vast the interior place becomes, the deeper the well becomes from which to draw peace—and the more available your soul is to wait in wonder.

Experiment this week:

Practice Active Waiting. This week, we will explore six activities to practice while waiting: giving back, acknowledging gratitude, taking baby steps, learning something new, getting into your body, and envisioning what you want or where you want to go. As you read through the reflections, try the corresponding activities. What other practices might these activities inspire? How can you cultivate these practices in your daily life during this season of waiting?

Giving Back

You received without payment;
give without payment.

–Matthew 10:8b

I can so easily shut down when I am waiting, focusing on my own situation. At my healthiest, I strive to take care of myself and get my needs met. But at worst, my world shrinks down to *my* situation, and I grow bored with myself!

One of my favorite fables is a story about a pearl. In one year a woman loses her husband and only child, a son. Unable to imagine anyone as devastated as herself, she visits the village sage, seeking his counsel for her grief. She climbs the mossy stairs to his mountain retreat and is greeted warmly at the door. "Come in, my sister," he says. "Come and sit with me a while and tell me about your terrible misfortune."

She takes a soft chair by the peat fire and, with a burst of tears, recounts her woes. All the while he listens, nods, and waits for her story to unfold.

When her sad tale finally runs its course, he sits back in his armchair, tents his hands, then places one on his heart. "My dear sister," he begins, "I am so sorry to hear of your loss and your pain. But I have a quest for you that will restore your joy."

The woman, astounded that she can feel even the slightest ray of hope, waits for his wise words, leaning in with anticipation.

"Many years ago," the sage says, "I lost a beautiful pearl. I still remember the heft of it in my hand and its luminescence to my eye. I am sure that someone has found it and even now holds onto it, waiting to return it to its rightful owner. I need for you to go in search of this pearl and bring it back to me. But as you go to each house, do not ask first for the pearl, for some may become defensive. First, enter the homes and listen to the woes of the people as I have listened to yours today."

So the woman sets out on the road, and at each house, she is welcomed in. She sits with people—some with large families, some who live alone—and listens to their stories. She nods, and *hmmms*, and cries with them. This goes on for a week, a month, a year. Eventually, the sting of her own pain passes into the joy of consoling others. She never finds the pearl, but she does find joy again.

In the midst of my own waiting, I remember the wisdom of this story and vow to give back in some way, focusing on needs outside myself. In this season of giving, I think about what I have to offer and of the precious gifts others have generously given me, especially when I couldn't reciprocate. Before long, in serving others, in giving back, my own pain diminishes, and I find myself reoriented and re-charged in the ability to wait.

THIRD TUESDAY OF ADVENT

Gratitude

*May you be made strong with all the strength
that comes from his glorious power,
and may you be prepared to endure everything
with patience, while joyfully giving thanks to
the Father who has enabled you to share in the
inheritance of the saints in the light.*

–Colossians 1:11-12

You've probably heard of the importance of cultivating "an attitude of gratitude." Unfortunately, whenever I hear that phrase or it pops into my mind, I seem to be in the midst of some irritating situation that I am not thankful for! Or I am wallowing in some little pity pit, and the words taunt me with snarkiness rather than hope.

But even when the words ring with annoyance, I try to listen to their wisdom. Often it is easier to get wound up by negativity. Our culture suffers from a pervasive pressure to focus on the bad news, to see one's self as a pawn or a victim, to feel put upon or assaulted by one thing after another.

Nevertheless, study after study shows that complaining and a negative outlook are bad for our health. These behaviors tax our physical, mental, and emotional systems.

While we can't always change our situation, the length of time that we may have to wait, or the people with whom we must interact, we can change our responses. We can control how we choose to be.

It pours rain outside as I write this meditation—sheets of water slicing from the sky. I am supposed to tour a college campus with my son, and then we have a long drive home—two things I am not excited about doing in the rain. But for now, I enjoy listening to the steady patter on the palms outside as I write. Goodness knows the parched earth needs this rain. Now the orange poppies will surely bloom on the hillsides, brightening my drive up the coast.

Last year I lived in London, a city notorious for its gloom and rain. I'm an American gal from the South who needs her sunshine, and I was concerned about the lack of daylight. So before moving to England, I invested in a pair of beautiful rain boots. Each time it rained, I looked forward to pulling on my awesome "wellies." It was grey outside, but my boots buoyed my mood.

Cultivating an attitude of gratitude: it's not a bad idea. What better season than Advent to shift focus from regretting what we don't have to loving the things that we do? It takes a mere shift in perspective and the choice to look for beauty and joy.

Baby Steps

*Therefore since we are justified by faith, we have peace
with God through our Lord Jesus Christ, through
whom we have obtained access to this grace in which
we stand; and we boast in our hope of sharing the
glory of God. And not only that, but we also boast
in our sufferings, knowing that suffering produces
endurance, and endurance produces character,
and character produces hope.*

–Romans 5:1-4

I am not a patient person. I admire those who are, but thus
far I have failed miserably in cultivating patience in myself.
I keep trying though, because I recognize that patience isn't
just about waiting; it's about *how* one waits. I cause myself an
inordinate amount of pain with my impatience. I would do well
to remember what philosopher Jean-Jacques Rousseau notes,
"Patience is bitter, but its fruit is sweet."[11]

---

11 Originally written by John Chardin, *Voyages en Perse et autres lieux de l'Orient* (1711).

There's a famous story about the Japanese auto manufacturer Toyota. American auto executives visited the Toyota plants to see how they were turning out so many more vehicles, with fewer errors, than other car manufacturing plants. What they found came to be known as the Toyota Production System, a constant, continuous effort at improvement by every worker at every level. Even on the assembly line, a riveter could shut down production if he or she saw a problem or a better way of doing something. Instead of merely adopting a new business model, Toyota, like so many Japanese businesses after World War II, adopted a new mindset—indeed a whole new philosophy.

The philosophy that became their core business principle was known as *kaizen*. Translated to English, *kaizen* means "good change" —constant, continuous improvement, or as I once heard it rendered, "baby steps."

On retreat once, I was taught the exercise of *kaizen* as baby steps. This is how it works: With a partner you commit to some new, improved behavior. Then you suggest how you will start practicing this behavior. Because most of us have inflated expectations of our willingness to change, we shoot too high with that first suggestion. The partner's job is to take us backward through simpler and simpler steps until we are taking the tiniest, most manageable, baby-est of steps. For example, my goal of getting more physically fit was reduced from working out at the gym, to first joining a gym, to finding out about joining a gym, to looking up the phone number for the gym. I could do that—Google the phone number. And I did.

Kaizen maintains the popular saying that big things can happen in small, incremental steps. Likewise, good character is not formed, new behavior is not assimilated, new perspective is not integrated overnight. These things are created little by little, moment to moment, with sweet little baby steps.

Learning

*Keep on doing the things that you have learned
and received and heard and seen in me,
and the God of peace will be with you.*

–Philippians 4:9

Our brains are hardwired to learn. From birth our minds are primed to take in data and create neural pathways to make sense of that information. As we mature, the pathways most used develop more and become stronger—like a grooved track. Even into old age, our miraculous brains remain "plastic" enough to create new connections.

When you learn something new, pleasure-wielding chemicals release into your brain. Synapses enlarge to receive chemical messages. And you literally feel the same pleasure you might by eating chocolate or having sex!

If you are learning something new as you read this reflection, multitudes of your neurons will change in about fifteen minutes, creating synapses and receptors. Stimulation releases a burst of activity, an electrical signal passes from the senses of taste, smell, sight, sound, and touch, releasing a chemical message through the synapse, locking onto the neuron on the other side. These chemical messages, or neurotransmitters, include "liquid keys" such as epinephrine, norepinephrine, glutamate, and GABA. They include serotonin and dopamine. Dopamine drives us, motivates us, and focuses us. The more dopamine released in the brain, the more reward centers are triggered. Activating reward circuits floods the brain with feelings of pleasure—and we crave pleasure! We crave this pleasurable dopamine boost so much that this is how addictions begin.[12]

Through creative outlets like writing, making things, reading, making music, or doing puzzles, our brains experience new sensations and set off this chain reaction of learning. Did you ever think that decorating cookies, making gifts, writing special cards, and singing new carols could create new circuits in your brain? As you expand your definition of learning, you broaden your awareness of how to bring a sense of well-being into your life. As you learn something new over time, waiting becomes transformative and productive.

---

12 Frances E. Jensen, MD with Amy Ellis Nutt, *The Teenage Brain: A Neuroscientist's Survival Guide to Raising Adolescents and Young Adults* (New York: HarperCollins Publishers, 2015), 47–58.

Embodiment

*Or do you not know that your bodies are temples of the
Holy Spirit, within you, which you have from God,
and that you are not your own?*

—1 Corinthians 6:19

Breathe in four counts. Hold for seven. Breathe out for eight.
Breathe in four counts. Hold for seven. Breathe out for eight. I
sit in *Sukhasana*—easy pose—in my yoga class, my back straight
and uplifted, my legs crossed, my hands relaxed and loose atop
my thighs. I am engaged in the 4-7-8 breathing exercise that
calms us physiologically through the vagus nerve, slowing the
heart rate. I am not thinking about anything else but my breath
and posture. I am here now, fully present in the moment and
fully present in my body.

I am not in my head, and that is a good thing! I dwell there
entirely too much. I need to get out of my head and the
relentless swirl of my thoughts, and this intentional way of
breathing is the best way I know how.

Too often Christianity becomes a religion of the head. But at its very essence, it is a relationship of the heart and body, where God makes a temple. In Jesus, God takes on mortal flesh—blood, bones, body, breath—needing food and drink, love and purpose. Christianity is nothing if not radically, at its very root, incarnate.

When we invite our bodies to waiting, the quality of our waiting shifts from passivity to activity. Whether that activity is holding a yoga pose or pounding the pavement jogging, walking a labyrinth or hiking in the woods, our hearts pump, our blood pulses through our veins, our breath deepens, and our pores open. Oxygen suffuses our brains, and endorphins course through our systems.

Saint Augustine once said, "It is solved by walking." Whether the full answer comes or if we gain some measure of resolution and well-being, renewed patience often accompanies physical engagement. Propelling the body through space triggers a sense of mental movement as well. It is hard to feel stuck when your body moves. Like our getting out of the way spiritually through contemplation, experiencing embodiment gets us out of our heads and thoughts and into our guts and souls.

Because Christianity has often reflected a dualistic relationship between spirit and flesh—a dualism particularly emphasized in Pauline theology—many believe that the religion denigrates the body, abases our human physicality. But this is a misunderstanding that disregards the unique salvific message of Christianity. God came into this world in the flesh because from the beginning, God created us as creatures of flesh and proclaimed that we are good. As we celebrate at Christmas, God comes to meet us in the flesh, reminding us that our bodies are temples for the Holy Spirit. Saint Paul professes that our minds, spirits, souls, and bodies remain intact in salvation. Each is constituent of the fullness of our salvation. We are not split apart into good substance and bad but wholly renewed because everything that God creates is good.

This truth may never be more evident than on Ash Wednesday when the mark of the cinder cross on our foreheads reminds us that we are dust and to dust we shall return. We are sealed by the Holy Spirit in baptism and marked as Christ's own forever—sharing in both his unconfused and inseparable divinity and humanity. And it is good.

THIRD SATURDAY OF ADVENT

Envisioning

Then I saw a new heaven and a new earth;
for the first heaven and the first earth had passed away,
and the sea was no more. And I saw the holy city,
the new Jerusalem, coming down out of heaven....
And I heard a loud voice from the throne saying,
"See the throne of God is among mortals. He will dwell with
them as their God; they will be his peoples, and God himself
will be with them; he will wipe every tear from their eyes.
Death will be no more; mourning and crying and pain will
be no more, for the first things have passed away."

–Revelation 21:1-4

As we wait and move through time, God moves ever toward us—working, creating, reconciling, and healing. With only days until we celebrate the birth of Jesus Christ, in the starlight of whom we are waiting, a community forms with others who also wait. We nourish a place within ourselves ready to receive the fullness of his radiance and power.

We end this week with six constructive ways to move toward and meet God on the way of waiting. Next week, we will focus on the theme of anticipation. Ideally these suggestions will foster a sense of anticipation while waiting, so that you can move through time more consciously. They are intended to help keep equilibrium even in the midst of confusion, crisis, and chaos, ascribing to your patience not only forbearance but also value, dignity, and merit.

Imagine what you truly want in your life, and hold onto that vision. Visualize what things will look like when you get there. What do you want? How will it feel? What are your relationships like there?

Allow yourself to feel a full range of emotions and accept your impatience and frustration at being obliged to wait. Stuffing or denying feelings won't make them go away. They just go underground or come out in ways that you don't always want them to or realize. Attune yourself to what gives you energy and what drains you. Pay attention to your dreams. The subconscious mind stores all our experiences—all that we have ever heard, said, seen, or read. This part has access to feelings and information beyond our surface awareness, continually sifting through, comparing, and processing them. While we are waiting, our subconscious minds work actively and tirelessly to make sense of our world and bring resolution.

Admit that your life is in process and arriving at a new state could take weeks, months, or years. The journey most likely will not be linear, and you may revisit similar places along the way.

(Certainly this has been the case in history as we have waited for 2,000 years for Christ to come again!) But each time, even though those places may feel the same, they are qualitatively different, and you bring new wisdom with you.

Look at waiting as a period of excavation or incubation. Open yourself to the idea that things are changing even when you cannot see or feel the movement. Such a stance acknowledges that others have a role to play in your drama as it unfolds. You don't and cannot know all the dynamics at work.

Remember that life's experiences—good or bad—provide material for learning. And remember that no experience—good or bad—need be wasted. Ask yourself: What does this failure, this fallow time, this moment of expectancy make possible?

Do whatever you need to work toward peace, health, patience, and wholeness. This week we have reflected on some ways to work toward peace, health, patience, and wholeness. Be gentle with yourself. Remember that your needs are as important as others'. You may need to put on your oxygen mask first before helping others with theirs. Claim what you need to feel peaceful, healthy, patient, and whole.

Anticipation

Anticipation arouses a cluster of emotions: excitement, enthusiasm, pleasure. Yet it can also elicit emotions like anxiety, trepidation, or fear. This fervent combination of emotions makes for a heady concoction. Anticipation titillates, fantasizes, and wishes. As French philosopher Albert Camus notes, "we need the sweet pain of anticipation to tell us we are really alive."

Based in our imaginative speculation, anticipation envisages what could be. The stronger the visualization, the more invested we can become in the projection. We can reduce stress and increase patience by envisioning what will be. By building a projection with our preferences, ideals, and desires, we can turn a negative "now" into a hopeful "yet to come."

In some cases, our imaginations, in their creative boundlessness, can be more charged than reality. Sometimes anticipation surpasses the feelings surrounding the actual event. I think about what Winnie the Pooh says in A. A. Milne's first classic volume: "'Well,' said Pooh, 'what I like best,' and then he had to stop and think. Because although eating honey was a very good thing to do, there was a moment just before you began to eat it which was better than when you were, but he didn't know what it was called."

Anticipation can heighten emotions in a negative way too. Sometimes worrying about an impending event can be worse than the actual thing when it happens. I know people who are undone by the prospect of public speaking or academic exams. But making the presentation or taking the test, when they came to pass, weren't really that bad. Usually having the news of what *is* relieves us from all the wild speculation of what *could be*. We can deal with reality, but it is often much harder to deal with the giants of our invention.[13] Whether anticipating something exciting or fearful, our imaginations often magnify emotions.

Anticipation. It can be so delicious, because, like Winnie the Pooh, we almost taste fulfillment in expectation. And it can be so excruciating—that aching, unrequited yearning. Whether in delight or yearning—by projecting into and believing in the future—anticipation trusts. It trusts by investing in the future, thus driving the present by infusing it with intention and possibility.

Anticipation defers gratification. Deferring gratification means taking time and making an effort to achieve something, or simply being willing to wait. This willingness shows that we value the thing we are anticipating.

---

13 See John Ohmer's great book on overcoming the giant anxieties and hurdles in our lives in *Slaying Your Goliaths: How God Can Help* (Cincinnati, Ohio: Forward Movement, 2015).

The combination of anticipation and deferral motivate us with a sense of purpose. As British psychotherapist and essayist Adam Phillips observes, to enjoy one's life, "one needs a belief in Time as a promising medium to do things in; one needs to be able to suffer the pains and pleasures of anticipation and deferral".[14]

In this fourth and final week, which expands and contracts according to the number of days in Advent, we look more immediately toward the birth of Christ and the anticipation of new life.

Experiment this week:

Check in with yourself. What do you need? How are you feeling in the Advent season? Stressed? Relaxed? Hopeful? Weary? Expectant? Disappointed?

Saint Ignatius of Loyola encouraged those he directed spiritually to bring all their senses to prayer and meditation. Take some time each day—two to five minutes, or longer if you can. Read the account of Jesus' birth in the Gospel of Luke. Imagine yourself there. What would it be like? How would it sound? What might you smell or taste? How does it feel?

At the end of your meditation, think about what stands out from the exercise. What do you notice? Say a short prayer about what you notice or about what causes you to wonder.

---

14 Adam Phillips, *On Flirtation* (London, 1994), 47.

Meaning and What Matters

For God so loved the world that he gave his only Son,
so that everyone who believes in him may not perish
but may have eternal life.

—John 3:16

In Fyodor Dostoevsky's epic novel *Crime and Punishment*, the anti-hero Raskolinikov is detached from the world and his own humanity. Incarcerated at a prison camp in Siberia for a brutal robbery and cold-blooded murder, he still can't quite understand why he is being punished for what he sees as mere transferal of wealth from a stingy old woman to himself, a student in need.

When he is shipped off, a young woman who loves him, Sonia Marmeladov, follows him to Siberia. Each day during his exercise break he hangs out by the prison fence, and Sonia comes to offer her company. Even though she has followed him there, brings him small gifts, and comes to see him every day, Raskolinikov remains cold to her cherishing warmth. If anything, he feels mild irritation. Unresponsive to her loving gestures, he hangs out at the fence—more out of boredom and something to do than out of affection toward Sonia.

In a turn of events, Sonia becomes ill and for several weeks is unable to visit. Raskolinikov, in her absence, loiters at the fence out of habit. When Sonia recovers, she sends word that she will be back at the usual spot. This day, as Raskolinikov wanders up and down, as if by a bolt of lightning, he realizes that he is not loitering and mooching with his typical indifference—he actually cares that Sonia is coming. He admits to himself that he is waiting for her. In waiting for her with anticipation, he realizes that he has missed her, that she matters to him. He values her company, and, indeed, loves her.

This story shows the connection between waiting and love. When we love something, we are willing to wait for it. When we care about someone, when we value them, when they matter to us, we will wait for them. We extend our love to them, in a most vulnerable, laid-open-bare way, and we wait for their response—of acceptance or rejection. As V.H. Vanstone notes in his book *The Stature of Waiting*, "When we love we hand ourselves over to receive from another our own triumph or our own tragedy."[15]

God comes into the world in the flesh, a defenseless babe. In this condition God reveals a self-emptying posture of love and fragility. God *so* loved that God reached out in intentional,

---

15 Much of this reflection is influenced by W.H. Vanstone's *The Stature of Waiting* (Harrison, Pennsylvania: Moorehouse Publishing, 1982). This quote is from page 96.

unguarded offering—willing even to suffer a response of indifference and rejection.

In this way, we mortals reflect the image of God who "so loved the world that he gave his only Son," so that all might be saved. When we wait, we acknowledge that something matters. Whether we wait on something as mundane as a test result or a red light or as sublime as a lover's first kiss or the birth of a child, we show a willingness to engage with the real, incarnate, messy world. Whether we wait for our daily bread or for God's kingdom to come, we imitate the divine waiting on this world, investing it with possibility and the power of meaning.[16]

---

16 Ibid, p. 109.

Loving with All

*In the beginning was the Word, and the Word was
with God, and the Word was God. He was in the
beginning with God. All things came into being
through him, and without him not one thing came
into being…And the Word became flesh and lived
among us, and we have seen his glory, the glory as of a
father's only son, full of grace and truth.*

John 1:1–3, 14

The French author Antoine de Saint-Exupery, author of *The
Little Prince*, was one of the greatest writers of the twentieth
century. He wrote only a few books before being killed while
flying reconnaissance missions during World War II. It seems
unlikely that such a great author would serve as a fighter pilot,
but he believed that he must serve God and country to the
fullest—heart, body, mind, and soul—and volunteered for the
most dangerous missions.

When a friend and colleague begged him to save himself for his
art, it is recorded that he replied, "Nobody has a right to write a

word today who does not participate to the fullest in the agony and trials of his fellow human beings. The Christian idea has to be served: That God's Word became flesh in love, and one must write one's love with one's body."

The Incarnation is about more than the birth of Jesus in a manger. As followers of a God who became flesh and dwelt among us, we are called to witness and serve in the world, writing with our bodies to narrate tomes of blessing by the living out of our lives. We are meant to live in this world and participate in the gritty realities of our own day.

God promises that a new Jerusalem will come down to this earth, and the earth and the heavens will be reconciled as one holy realm. The ushering in of the New Jerusalem began with Jesus' birth, life, death, and resurrection. And in this age, we await the return of Jesus for the consummation of the cosmos—the age when all will be in all. From the ordinary to the extraordinary we wait in the tension of these two times—the Alpha and the Omega.

FOURTH WEDNESDAY OF ADVENT

Possibility

*And all of us, with unveiled faces, seeing the glory
of the Lord as though reflected in a mirror,
are being transformed into the same image
from one degree of glory to another.*

–2 Corinthians 3:18a

I am curious to see how someone might describe me in twenty-five words or less—or tweet-length, perhaps. Would they focus on physical attributes or behavioral qualities? What choice labels would be used to elicit a cascade of associations?

We use labels to make sense of our world. Labeling can be helpful. Labels give useful ways to understand people. From our primal roots, labeling has proved an important way to quickly categorize someone as friend or foe.

But labeling can oversimplify and overstate another's characteristics or attributes. We tend to stereotype and assign attributes to others based on our past experiences rather than who they really are and what they are actually like. Not all rich people are the same, nor are all poor people. White and black, straight and gay, Episcopalian and Baptist: No group can be categorically labelled en masse.

When we classify in this way, labeling acts like a freeze frame—a limited perspective in a singular moment. When this freeze frame gains power in us, we deaden our ability to deal with others curiously, creatively, and sensitively. We diminish our courage to challenge the status quo and dismantle systemic bigotry.

For generations, the prophets foretold the coming of the Messiah who would overturn systems that diminish humanity; at great risk they boldly criticized the powers that be and persecution that was based in prejudice. Challenging and empowering, their words call upon all who feel lumped together because of labels to rise up against systems that reduce, diminish, and dehumanize. The prophets call on followers of a Messiah to become people of a different way—a way that promotes the flourishing of each of us, one that looks beyond labels to the dignity of every human being.

The biblical story is one of people overcoming potentially limiting labels. Moses, a stutterer, becomes the spokesperson for the people of Israel. Mary, at first an unwed mother, becomes the bearer of the awaited Messiah. Jesus, the carpenter's son, is the Son of God.

Resisting the urge to label encourages a broader perspective as we conform ourselves to Christ. Even if we see ourselves as coming from a place of brokenness or disgrace, we can be moving toward the possibility of wholeness and grace.

We have the opportunity to recast the time of waiting—this time in between what is and what is to come—as our own period of coming into possibility, to become the person we were created to be in God's eyes.

FOURTH THURSDAY OF ADVENT

In-Between

Thy kingdom come, thy will be done,
on earth as it is in heaven...
—The Lord's Prayer

It seems like I have preached on Trinity Sunday every year of my ordained ministry. Each time, I have refused to shy away from tackling the doctrine of the Trinity. Maybe at my own peril, I have tried to make sense out of a mystery that defies language and comparisons. Traditionally expounded, the doctrine upholds that God's nature is one unified whole known to us in three persons. This word "persons" derives from the Greek idea of *persona,* which is a dramatic term for a role, a manifestation of a certain character.

This ancient formulation of the Trinity focuses on the three entities known as one. But more contemporary formulations focus on the interactions between the three persons. They suggest an active, relational understanding of the Trinity. In essence, these less static explanations describe how the building blocks (persons) plus their interactions (love, reconciliation, apprehension of the other, creation, bringing forth the realization of the other's fullness) equal their relationship.

At our best, we mortals operate in this same way, mirroring the activity of God. We, the building blocks, plus our interactions (how we act with each other) determine the character, quality, and substance of our relationships. How we are in the space and time in between us constitutes the relationship. In other words, it's not what we say or our intentions that make up the relationship; it's what we actually do.

I want to bracket a comment here about intentions. The old saw says that the road to hell is paved with good intentions. That may be. But the road to heaven is too. What we intend matters. The direction in which we point ourselves has importance. Our intentions can direct our actions. The problem arises when intentions lose a sense of anticipation—when they no longer anticipate our actions.

In this season of Advent, as we await the birth and coming again of our newborn king, we attune ourselves to the sanctity of the in-between. We celebrate the mystery in between this age and the age to come. We contemplate what it means to live in between the events of Jesus' life—between birth and resurrection. We experience life lived in between the First Coming and the Final Coming, in between the Incarnation and the Consummation, in between this world and the New Jerusalem.

We feel the ache of anticipation, because God's intention is that in time, the in-between space will collapse, and we will be made whole. And so we pray, "thy kingdom come, thy will be done on earth as it is in heaven." We pray not that we will ascend and be taken up into some pie-in-the-sky paradise but that paradise comes on earth as it is in heaven. This world, in all its brokenness and beauty, misery and majesty becomes the locus of God's perfect intention made actual.

For this perfection we wait with anticipation.

Superpower

And now faith, hope, and love abide, these three;
and the greatest of these is love.

–1 Corinthians 13:13

Love. In the English language the word is used so often in so many ways for so many things that it loses its power to pack a punch. But in truth, there is nothing more powerful than love.

Love overcomes animosity, anxiety, and acrimony. It neutralizes devastation, degradation, and disgrace. It reverses hostility, hollowness, and hatred.

Anyone can love. Sure, we all have barriers to loving fully. Even in the most extreme cases of psychopathology and woundedness, one can still act with loving intent. One can choose the loving gesture, to act lovingly because God loves through us.

Love begets love. We love because we are first loved. Your love extended opens up the other to receive that love. Receiving that love opens the possibility of love returned and of love passed on. And then love abounds!

Love is your superpower.[17] Maybe you have others too: an ear for music, a heart for listening, a fortitude for surviving and thriving, a patience to wait, a curiosity to anticipate. These are wonderful, wealthy gifts. Yet whether you feel an abundance or a dearth of gifts, you have love as a superpower—all yours, should you choose to accept it.

It's there for the taking. Receiving it means to start by loving yourself—all the bumpy, rough, embarrassing, and messy bits mixed in with the admirable, fierce, and particular traits that make you in the image of God. Love is there for sharing with anyone you encounter—the irritating family member, the resentful sales clerk, the tailgating driver. It's there for extending to every being in God's marvelous universe—neighbors nearby and people at great distance; creatures creeping, crawling, swimming, and flying; plants majestic and miniscule; this planet earth and all creation.

Like the rivers flowing out of the temple in the vision of Ezekiel (chapter 47), your love can flow from you—the temple of the Holy Spirit—out through the sanctuary of your heart, through the doors of your mouth, and down the stairs of your life. It can flow out to the courtyard and into the marketplace of your community, to the gates of the city and beyond: great torrents of living waters bathing and baptizing the world in love.

---

17 This reflection is dedicated to Buddy Macuha, who is teaching me new and powerful things about love through the practice of yoga.

Love is your superpower today and every day. As we approach the celebration of love incarnate born into the world, let our hearts turn to that love, that we might bear it in the world.

Birth Pangs

*When a woman is in labor, she has pain, because her
hour has come. But when her child is born, she no
longer remembers the anguish because of the joy of
having brought a human being into the world.*

—John 16:21

You have arrived at the eve before the Christ-mass. Most likely
your anticipation has grown as you have counted off the four
weeks of Advent. The celebration of new birth awaits. That
you have made it to this point attests to the fact that there is
movement in waiting.

Holiday planning may have reached a fevered pitch or maybe
you have eased into the sweet spot where all that can be
done has been done. Now you wait for the mysterious eve of
Christmas to usher in that glorious day of new birth. On that
cusp, we all await the birth of Christ.

My labor pains with my first child began after sundown.
Contractions continued through the night and into the
eve of the following day. Much of my birthing was done in
the darkness.

In Western culture, we typically think of darkness in negative terms. Darkness is a place of threat, fear, evil. But there can be no light without darkness. It is out of darkness that light shines. Shadows mold our environments, giving dimension and form to reality. Dark places contour the light places in our lives.

Creation begins in darkness. The heavens are separated from the earth, the stars and heavenly bodies stake their course, creeping, crawling things emerge and swimming creatures swirl, beasts issue forth, and the formation of mortals begins after sunset. "And there was evening, and there was morning, the first day," Genesis tells us. God creates in the darkness.

The seed sprouts from the dark loam, the child emerges from the darkness of the womb, the eastern sun shines first from a dark horizon. These phenomena remind us that we may not be able to see what God is doing in the midst of dark and difficult situations. The creative truth of darkness reveals that when we think we are in a dead-end rut, deadlocked in conflict or deadened by lack of hope, God continually works to bring light and new life. The deep and dark realms of the subconscious sift, probe, process, and file experiences, collating them with past and present impulses to recalibrate new meaning.

As those new ideas come forth, in the hope of their revised vision, our souls rejoice. The pain of gestation and labor subsides. Anguish gives way to relief, release, opportunity, and holy promise.

CHRISTMAS DAY

O Great Mystery

O great mystery,
and wonderful sacrament,
that animals should see the new-born Lord,
lying in a manger!
Blessed is the Virgin whose womb
was worthy to bear
Christ the Lord.
Alleluia!

These words represent the English translation from the Latin text of *O Magnum Mysterium*, a responsorial chant sung at the Matins (Daily Office) service on Christmas morning. While most of the Christian world opens wrapped gifts and empties hearth-hung stockings, these sublime words, sung to the heavens in prayer, recall the miraculous birth of God incarnate into the world.

O great mystery!
O wonderful sacrament!

Into a small village in occupied Palestine, in a humble manger the awaited Messiah arrives. To an unwed mother under scandalous conditions the king of kings crowns.

O great mystery!
O wonderful sacrament!

Into the midst of burdensome taxation and the crushing of the poor, into the terrorism of Herod's slaughter of the innocents, into conditions of slavery, trafficking, war, floods, drought, and betrayal, God comes offering more. Birth. New life. Hope staked in flesh and blood. Liberation. Love. For the Christ is born into the world to be received and to dwell in the humble mangers of our hearts.

O great mystery!
O wonderful sacrament!

For as the Virgin's womb was worthy to bear Christ the Lord, so we mortals are worthy to bear Christ in the world. Our waiting in our own periods of gestation bears the fruit of her womb then, now, and to come.

O great mystery!
O wonderful sacrament!

On this day, and each day anew, amidst the braying and the rustle of hay, Christ the savior is born. Christ the savior is born.

ACKNOWLEDGEMENTS

I want to express deep gratitude to Forward Movement, which seems to reach out to me to write at the most opportune and critical times for my own soul work. I give thanks to the communities that have formed my theological thought through their teaching and allowing me to minister with them: the University of Virginia and Berkeley Divinity School at Yale; Christ Church, Greenwich; St. Paul's, Fairfield; Christ Church, New Haven; St. Bartholomew's Church, New York City; St. Luke's, San Francisco; Grace Cathedral, San Francisco; St. Mary the Virgin, San Francisco; and St. Paul's, London. I appreciate the patience of my friends and my family, David, Liam, and Rhea McSpadden. And finally, and ultimately, to the Holy Spirit who keeps me waiting and hoping in more.

About the Author

A graduate of Berkeley Divinity School at Yale and the University of Virginia, Christine McSpadden is an Episcopal priest and has served congregations from New York City to San Francisco to London. She regularly writes for Forward Movement and contributions include *Observing Lent* and *Resurrection Living* and meditations in *Soul Proclamations: Singing the Magnificat with Mary, The Bible Challenge* series, and *Forward Day by Day.*

About Forward Movement

Forward Movement is committed to inspiring disciples and empowering evangelists. While we produce great resources like this book, Forward Movement is not a publishing company. We are a ministry.

Our mission is to support you in your spiritual journey, to help you grow as a follower of Jesus Christ. Publishing books, daily reflections, studies for small groups, and online resources is an important way that we live out this ministry. More than a half million people read our daily devotions through *Forward Day by Day*, which is also available in Spanish (*Adelante Día a Día*) and Braille, online, as a podcast, and as an app for your smartphones or tablets. It is mailed to more than fifty countries, and we donate nearly 30,000 copies each quarter to prisons, hospitals, and nursing homes. We actively seek partners across the Church and look for ways to provide resources that inspire and challenge.

A ministry of The Episcopal Church for eighty years, Forward Movement is a nonprofit organization funded by sales of resources and gifts from generous donors. To learn more about Forward Movement and our resources, please visit us at www.forwardmovement.org (or www.venadelante.org).

We are delighted to be doing this work and invite your prayers and support.